JOHN LAWS
BOOK OF
IRREVERENT
LOGIC

Mike Hart
Mar. 1998

JOHN LAWS' BOOK OF IRREVERENT LOGIC

PAN
AUSTRALIA

First published in Pan in 1994
by Pan Macmillan Australia Pty Limited
63-71 Balfour Street, Chippendale, Sydney

Reprinted 1994

National Library of Australia
cataloguing-in-publication data:

       Laws, John, 1935-
       John Laws' book of irreverent logic.

       ISBN 0 330 35604 6

       1. Aphorisms and apothegms.
       2. Quotations, English, I. Title. II. Title: Book of irreverent logic.

       082

Design and finished art by Hugonnet Bouda Graphic Design
Printed in Australia by McPherson's Printing Group

JOHN LAWS' BOOK OF IRREVERENT LOGIC

*This book is in memory
of my friend Roger Miller.*

Introduction

This is a book of things I've heard and things I've said, things I've
thought and things I've read, statements I've made for which I may
well have been castigated, and some, dear reader, for which I may
have even been applauded - although I must admit my ears aren't
exactly ringing with the sound.

I hope these little notations, thoughts, comments, lines of stupidity
- however you may read them - have some effect on you. Some, I
know, will annoy you. Some, I know, will cause you to say: "now
wait a minute, you can't say *that*" . But of course, you *can* say that...
if you are irreverently logical.

How these many and varied attitudes came to me, I don't know -
but to anyone who contributed, directly or indirectly, I thank you.
My life has always been affected by people. People who have made
me sad, made me angry... people who have affected me in all sorts of
ways. These people are the catalyst for the thoughts that follow on
these pages. I have been fortunate to be able to publish the book
under the full understanding that if my name had not been John
Laws, it would not have been possible.

So I need to thank all the people who listen to my radio programme,
in more than a thousand towns and cities around Australia, for just
that - for allowing me to be John Laws.

John Laws, July 1994.

Keeping the Dream Alive

he "Keeping the Dream Alive Story" as it's known to pupils in the School of Irreverent Logic came really from I know not where. It came to me in dribs and drabs. After one day on radio I started to recall parts of it. A line had come from here, a line had come from there. I suspect it may have been put together in its pure form by Paul Harvey, respected American journalist, so Mr. Harvey if there is a bit of you in here, I hope I represent you properly. I assure you there is a lot of me. More importantly, there is a lot of everybody and a lot of truth.

Keeping the dream alive is all about hope for the next generation, and the generation after that - our children, our grandchildren, our great-grandchildren.

I'd really like for them to know about hand-me-down clothes and home-made ice-cream and leftover meat-loaf. My grandsons, I hope you learn humility by being humiliated. I hope you learn honesty by being cheated. I hope you learn to make your own bed, to mow the lawns, wash the car. I hope nobody gives you a brand new motor car when you're 17. I hope you have a job by then. It will be good at least one time if you see a baby lamb born or see your old dog put to sleep. I hope you get a black eye fighting for something that you believe in. I hope you have to share a bedroom with your younger brother - by the way it's alright to draw a line down the middle of the room. When he wants to crawl under the covers with you because he's scared, I hope you let him. I hope you have to walk uphill to school with your friends and I hope you live in a town where you can do it safely. I hope you learn to dig in dirt. I hope you learn to play marbles and read books and I hope when you learn those new-fangled computers you also learn how to add up and subtract in your bright little mind. I hope your friends give you a bad time when you have your first girlfriend, and I hope when you talk back to your mother you'll learn the taste of soap. I hope you skin your knee climbing mountains and burn your hand on the iron. May you feel

Keeping the Dream Alive

sorrow at a funeral and may you feel absolute happiness on your birthday. I hope your mother punishes you when you throw a cricket ball through a neighbour's window and I hope she hugs and kisses you at Christmas time when you buy her a bottle of the worst perfume money can buy.

These things I wish for you, tough times and disappointment, hard work and happiness.

completely well-adjusted person is a bore.

*A dream home is a myth;
a dream house is a slight possibility.*

A piece in the New York Times
*the other day: In 1943 there were exactly
44 homicides by gunshot in New York City.
In 1994, 1499 - and they tell you nothing is
wrong. According to the National Rifle
Association of America, more people die in motor
cars than by gunshots. I presume what they are
advocating is that we have more accurate cars.*

A political party that is truly socialistic is economically parasitic, using its political potency and its taxing authority to permit, no dear reader, even encourage one group of people to survive by the virtue of another.

A simple way to get votes:
Find something the Australian people haven't got,
tell them they have a right to have it -
and then promise to get it for them.

A society that loses its sense of outrage is doomed to extinction.

woman must have something on
- or there's nothing to take off.

Alexander the Great was the first pupil of Aristotle. Aristotle was the world's first school teacher. He would only teach school out of doors and all students were required to be on first name terms with Mother Nature.
Love fresh air and keep your strength of character and you will never be out of work.

All the supposed free thinkers of the world who constantly talk about change are really mind - manacled themselves. All they want to do is change others.

All I saw during the sexual revolution was a little hand-to-hand combat.
- C.R.

An absolutely balanced person is a candidate for the freak farm.

Born Before 1950

his piece has been around forever, even before 1950 - probably before 1940. One day it will probably appear in a form about being born before 1980. It comes out in various guises, in various places, at various times; only the dates are changed, so as not to incriminate the elderly. It gets added to, subtracted from - and I'll do precisely that again, dear reader, but it still makes interesting reading. Whether it means we've progressed or regressed, of course, is entirely up to you.

This is for all those born prior to 1950. We are the survivors. Consider the changes that we have witnessed: We were born before televisions, before penicillin, before polio shots, frozen foods, Xerox, contact lenses, frisbees and the pill. We were before radar, credit cards, laser beams, ball point pens, before pantihose, dishwashers, clothes driers, electric blankets, air conditioners, drip dry clothing and before man walked on the moon. We got married first and then lived together; today that's the wrong way round.

We were pre de-facto, gay rights, computer dating, duel careers and computer marriages. We were before day care centres, group therapy, nursing homes and councillors. We never heard of FM radio, television, tape decks, walkmans, word processors, artificial hearts, micro cassettes, yoghurt, blokes wearing earrings and girls putting them in their noses. A chip was a piece of wood used to heat water for a bath, hardware meant hammers, nails, good things to make things - and software didn't even exist back then.

Made in Japan meant junk and the term 'making out' meant how you did on your first day at work. Pizzas, McDonalds, instant coffee, tea bags and towelettes meant nothing. Chicken was a luxury at Christmas after Dad cut the head off one of the chooks and Mum had spent hours plucking it. A battery was just something you put in a torch or to start your car.

Born Before 1950

Cigarette smoking was fashionable, grass was mown, coke was a cold drink and pot was something you cooked in. Rock music was Brahms' Lullaby, Aids were sort of nice ladies in white who visited your Grandma, and a crack salesman was a man who sold alot of brushes for Mr Fuller. Boys were boys and girls were girls - we never knew you had a choice. Gay was just what our hearts were. There was only one way to get money - work and it wasn't a dirty word. And maybe we were the last generation to think you needed a husband to have a baby.

No wonder we're so confused.

 *nybody can die;*
it's the coming back that's the real challenge.

ren't you getting tired of the individuals and groups who claim to be politically correct, who preach tolerance, but fail to practice it. They believe that nobody can possibly disagree with them, even for the most honest of reasons. What they're asking us to tolerate, of course, is their own intolerance.

rt is life, so the bad *artists tell you.*
The thing is of course that you can
turn your back on art.

As you know, dear reader,
I often think about the politically correct.
Isn't it hard to take somebody seriously,
who is so fussy about stupid little things,
like avoiding such words as chairman
or mankind? Big thinkers, eh?

*Interesting fact -
sponges grow in the ocean.
I wonder how much deeper the ocean
would be if that didn't happen.*

e brave enough to say something is good.

e more *aware of your responsibility*
than you are of your rights.

Be thankful - if you didn't have a nose, you'd have to stick your ear in other people's business.

ecause I didn't work when I was at school I had to use my brains when I wasn't.

*Behind every successful man
is a not so successful man trying to
bring him down.*

*Being free of pretence does not mean
you are in touch with the truth.
Sincerity is not proof of the truth.*

Farmers

f you hear some-
body criticise a
farmer, stop him
quickly. Farmers
are indispensable
and we know it or
we used to know it. How the world
has changed, because of the do-
gooders, particularly the environazis, the watermelons, i.e. green on
the outside, red on the inside. These
are the malcontents who seem to see
farmers as some sort of marauders
of the environment. How wrong they
are, dear reader, how wrong they
are.

When I was growing up farmers
were good men and their families
good people. If you were at school with
the son of a grazier and he was your
friend, you were in great shape, and
if your sister was going to marry the
son of a grazier, you were in even
better shape, not to mention her
status on the social ladder. She's
marrying a man on the land, gentry
or otherwise - he was a man on the
land.

You see they weren't called farmers
to much back then. They were men
on the land. What they really were,
and of course are, is the land, people
of the soil, the ones who maintain
the true pioneer spirit that makes
Australia the best. And they were
everywhere, not just on the land.
They were in Parliament, Federal
and State, they were on Councils,
they organised charities, some even
left the land temporarily, but only
temporarily (people only ever leave
the land temporarily) to become
lawyers, or physicians, but their
properties were their priorities, their
homes and always their first love.

A lot of great ideas, a lot of
outstanding leadership has come by
way of farmers and it's not too hard
to work out why. Just think about
it. Farming would have to be
conducive to creativity, to imagination, certainly to initiative.
Working hard in the soil, the quiet
of the bush, farmers think, and
think deeply, about many, many
things. They enjoy the luxury of
tranquillity frequently but maybe
not frequently enough.

Farmers

They rarely stop working, they rarely stop thinking for that matter, they don't stop even on rainy days. They don't stop. You don't just sit around, you do things - the overdue mechanical jobs, you tidy up the shed. Of course it never looks tidy and it never will and you know it. But then come the clear days sitting on a tractor, concentrating on a straight line, working your way towards the middle, the mind works its way to the middle of problems - maybe the future of the country, maybe human rights, but something good, something substantive, something noble. Farmers are noble thinkers.

Why aren't all these nuisance feminazis supporting the farmers of the world? If ever there was an equal opportunity employer, this is one, dear reader. Since time in memoriam, it's been a fact, the farmer's wife has equal rights and sometimes more participation in the operation of the place. There are no thought police, or do-gooders, to stop them from driving a tractor, milking a cow, throwing out the hay, picking the vegetables, or anything

they want to do for that matter. It's true, dear reader, since the dawn of agriculture, the farmer has been the foremost example of equal opportunity.

I said farmers are indispensable and I mean, indispensable. This is an undeniable fact. You could live without me - I'm just a thinker. You could probably get by without journalists, you would survive without a banker, a lawyer, but you can't survive without food. Where does the food come from? Farmers. That's it, farmers.

So farmers are a central part of survival but sadly we no longer give them the respect to which they should be entitled. Once we looked up, now many look down, to the farmer, the grazier, the man on the land. Stop, look and listen. There is not a city in the nation that doesn't have it's daily reports of murders, rape, poverty, homelessness. Surely that's proof positive that people in the city aren't better than people in the country.

Farmers

The bambi-brigade, the friends of fur and feather, the environazis (the extremists in other words), attack the farmer. He uses fertilisers, he uses pesticides. Maybe he does, maybe he doesn't. But he produces sufficient food to feed the fanatics and anybody else who has a desire to survive.

If the tiniest little puddle of water suddenly appears in the middle of his most prosperous paddock, you can bet "London to a brick", as Ken Howard used to say, that some half-wit will appeal to some other half-wit, and given that he is a half-wit, he will more than likely know a bureaucrat or someone in government, and before you know it the prosperous paddock is proclaimed a wetland. Finish, they prohibit the farmer from touching it.

It's no easy life. Think about the tobacco farmers, dear reader. They are now the subject of ridicule, abuse, picketing, or any other sort of damn fool behaviour that these do-gooders get up to, as the tobacco farmers grow the dreaded weed. If the same old farmer had decided to grow peanuts instead of tobacco, he would still be in trouble for clogging up the world's arteries. If he ploughs all that back into the ground and goes for beef cattle and pigs (heaven forbid), then he is in trouble for over populating the land and creating methane gas to destroy the ozone layer because the cows, or the pigs, have the temerity to break wind.

And let's not even talk about the egg farmer. This poor hard worker, the egg farmer, was nearly put out of business when the foodies, those from the lentil institutions, decided that eggs were to blame for high cholesterol. Of course, now they have changed their minds. No apologies mind you. No-one held responsible for the near death of an industry. The same of course, with the apple. They damned nearly killed that industry too with the scare about Alar. Remember Meryl Streep appearing before the American Senators telling the world that Alar causes cancer. Why is it that in order to be politically correct, we take the word of some

Farmers

film actress over and above the word of scientists? This is what the do-gooders have done for us.

Once upon a time, dear reader, when this place was Australia and brave, strong men of almost any age, conquered the seemingly unconquerable outback and had it teeming with livestock. Absolutely teeming - horses, cattle, sheep. The place was rich, monetarily and spiritually.

Now you have the raving do-gooders saying that livestock destroys the environment. Wasn't it horses and livestock that made the great environment that used to be the great Australia? Wasn't it men and horses who survived - tamed this violent land?

If you happen to be a do-gooder reading this book (and we've had it published in its brown wrapper so you can read it without fear of assassination) could you tell us what you would like the farmer to do? Give him a break will you. Give him a break. It would serve us all right if the farmers parked the tractors, handed in their hoes, eradicated their livestock, gave what was left to the starving masses in the Third World and told the do-gooders to go grow their own watercress.

I wonder how long they would last.

*Being poor isn't all that bad.
At least you know what you can do without,
so you're a whole lot better off than somebody
who's always had it and can't imagine what
it would be like to do without it.*

eware of what the politically
correct call "learning experiences", i.e. I made
a terrible mistake but it was a "learning
experience". Quite often "learning experiences"
are paid for with the sacrifice of standards.
The only learning experience that is
worthwhile is the one that teaches you
something of value.

Beware of the fanatical search
for social justice in extremes. Extremists,
of course, never think they're extreme.
The spectre of social justice, along with religion,
maintains the greatest applicability with misery.

*hristianity and church-going
should not be confused.*

*If you're not the lead dog,
the view never changes.*

*Communes don't work
and will NEVER work.*

One hundred percent of all non smokers die.

*ount your enemies.
If you haven't got any, chances are
you haven't got any friends either.*

Don't spoil your chances for a large increase by asking for a small one.

Never ask in a book store
where the self help section is,
it defeats the whole purpose.

Don't stand still;
it's the same as going backwards.

Little Towns

omebody once sent me a newspaper clipping about little towns. It didn't mean a great deal to me at the time, because I'd spent a lot of time in little towns and I regarded what was said in that clipping as being no more than fact, and thought that it would be of precious little interest to city folk. How wrong I was. I recorded it, or what I could remember of it. Since then I've probably had more requests for that piece than anything else I've done on radio.

It originally came out of an American newspaper in Oklahoma. I remember the name of the paper because that alone impressed me. It was called The Daily Citizen. "Citizen" - a word not used much these days, a fine word. Try to be a good one. Anyway, let me give you the little town story, from my memory.

A little town is where everybody knows what everybody else is doing. They don't talk about it too much, but they do check the newspapers just to see who got caught.

In a little town your neighbour knows what time you leave in the morning and what time you're home at night without even opening his eyes; he can tell by the sound of your car. And he not only knows when the car goes, he knows where it goes. The chances are, if he didn't hear it come home at the expected time one night, he would sit up in bed and say, what was that!

If you live in a little town you are wasting your time telling fibs about your age, or your ailments, or your ancestors.

A little town is where if you get a wrong number you can talk as long as you like, if you want to. And in the good old days when yours was one long and two short and theirs was two short and one long, you could listen in if you wanted to - but you rarely heard something you didn't already know.

Little Towns

A little town is where there's hardly anything to do, but nobody's ever got enough time to do it anyway.

In any old town, you'll probably find one bad person, to every hundred good. In a big town the good people feel uncomfortable. In a little town the bad people feel uncomfortable.

Little towns have Lions Clubs, Chambers of Commerce, Apex, Rotary and the rest, and all the businessmen support everything they can. They'll help nearly everybody and yet nearly everyone goes to the big town to do their shopping.

When they gossip in the small towns, they kind of cut down anybody who's up, but they quickly help up anybody who's down.

A small town policeman has a first name. A small town school teacher has the last word. The small town clergy is often a full-time coach. As for the fireman in a small town... that's everybody.

IN A LITTLE TOWN GAOL THERE'S RARELY ANYBODY; AND IN THE TOWN CEMETERY YOU'RE ALWAYS AMONG FRIENDS.

And now, dear reader, I hear you ask: why would anybody want to live in one of these teenzie weenzie, sneeze-and-you-miss-it towns? Oh, I think that somehow there are lots of reasons. In the school play there's a part for everybody; in the town gaol there's rarely anybody; and in the town cemetery you're always among friends.

Thanks to The Daily Citizen - *if you are still alive and well. I hope I did your piece justice.*

Don't gossip.
If you don't see it, don't say it.

Drunk? Why not?
What the sober man has in his heart,
the drunken man puts on paper.

*Eat, drink –
and be fat and drunk.*

*quality used to be just that.
Equality. Treating everyone equally, alike.
These days that's not it at all.
Equality now means discrimination disguised
as ideals; it means preferential treatment
for special interest groups, including women.
We should start to think about this while
we are still allowed to.*

Everybody has the right to be left alone but nobody has the right to demand approval.

xercise your right not to exercise.

*enerally speaking,
the less government has an entanglement
in things, particularly families,
the better they work.
There are certain areas in which
autonomy is paramount
- and the family is one.*

God made *Adam* first just because he didn't want any advice on how to.

overnment is not the solution.
Government is only part of the solution.
People are the solution.

Government spending
is not compassion. Government spending
of the taxpayers' money has nothing to do with
compassion. Showing compassion by giving away
somebody else's money? You're kidding!

Governments shouldn't be a first resource - they should be a last resort.

The Vandals who Change History

here are people in the world who are of the misguided opinion that we should lead totally undisrupted lives. There must be no worries, no concern, no heartbreak, no poverty, no extremes of any sort. The people who subscribe to this theory, and encourage it, are generally the *non-achievers*. Even worse they are ignorant of the real mystery of being. If you've enjoyed a little and endured much, you've done well.

You will find most people who have made their mark, or are on their way to making their mark in life, have had their ups and downs. They've enjoyed a little and endured a lot. If it wasn't for the downs, you would never really appreciate the ups - and that's where these morally anointed do-gooding, self-righteous sycophants, these parasites of society, these pariahs of personal responsibility, have got it all wrong.

They believe one little problem, one little mistake, one little down and you are entitled to victim status. If you lose your job, you must be told it wasn't your fault. If you murder your mother, you must also be told it wasn't your fault. You require, what we now affectionately know and sadly accept, as counselling - the greatest growth industry of the nineties. Counselling kills personal responsibility.

IF YOU'VE ENJOYED A LITTLE AND ENDURED MUCH, YOU'VE DONE WELL.

These are the people who tell, those dumb enough to listen, that the world is always good - no highs, no lows - just always good. Well, I've got news for you, dear reader; the world isn't always good. Life can be a bitch, as some now-forgotten spruiker of "new-speak" said recently. He or she was right; life can be a bitch.

It's confronting this fact and dealing with it that makes life worthwhile. It's overcoming this challenge that makes you a success - not a failure, and not a nothing wallowing in self-pity - comfortable in the belief that

The Vandals who Change History

somebody caused your trouble, not you, but someone else... because the do-gooders told you so.

It's out of control; it's gone too far. By swallowing this politically correct nonsense, we have lied to ourselves and we are lying to our children - shame on us. The Politically Correct have got hold of the language and distorted it to such a degree that we now lie to ourselves. They even want to change history, and that's exactly what they're doing, changing history and history is one of the most remarkable things in our lives. The mere fact that it happened is remarkable. Some was good, some was bad, some was bar-baric, some was humane, some was horrible beyond belief... a lot was very romantic. Much of it in fact so extraordinary that you could think it to be fiction. It's not, it's fact... or it used to be.

> HISTORY IS ONE OF THE MOST REMARKABLE THINGS IN OUR LIVES. THE MERE FACT THAT IT HAPPENED IS REMARKABLE.

Recently the New South Wales Board of Studies and the Queensland Board of Studies decided that we, the majority of Australians (about 98 percent of us who are not aboriginal), didn't "settle" in this country, didn't "discover" this country. We "invaded" it. The reason that the 98 percent now have to be known as invaders is because we couldn't possibly upset the two percent. This, of course, is simply divisive. It makes the two percent dislike us even more. We didn't just discover the place, we invaded it. The definition of "invade" is "to enter a country by military force", "to enter as an enemy, go into with hostile intent".

This society is becoming so saturated, so absorbed with lies, we don't know how to ring out the truth anymore. Some will say they are simply adding to the truth. But if you add to the truth, you subtract from it.

Have you ever noticed, dear reader,
that some medicine bottle caps are on so tight
that if you're strong enough to get them off,
you're probably not sick at all.

*Have you ever noticed that if
you have a different point of view to an extremist
you are immediately a bigot?*

*He who is unaware of ignorance
can only be misled by his knowledge.*

omophobia, one of the most
misused words of newspeak, or lunatic language
as I call it, only means fear of homosexuals when
the frightened person is himself a homosexual.
See what I mean about distorting
the fact to suit the occasion.

Horse racing, we are told
is the Sport of Kings. So drag racing must
be the Sport of Queens.

*How old? Fifty-ish...
give or take an "ish".*
- B.B.

*Why are people always claiming
things are untouched by human hands?
What the hell's wrong with human hands?
Can you mention a better kind?*

'd rather brush with ordinary toothpaste and have 21 percent fewer commercials.

don't care what the hell you *

* *Please colour your own heart red.*
This is our colouring-in page.

I have made plenty for myself in my life but more importantly I've helped others make fortunes.

I know how we could bring down
the deficit and so does the government.
They **won't** do it and I **can't** - but it's very easy:
just get rid of all the fool counter-productive,
interfering, government programmes, and there
are plenty of them. That would be the easy part;
the hard part would be getting re-elected
- and that, friends, is why they won't do it.

The Truth Stealers

hen you were a young one, you may have read The Billabong Books, written by Mary Grant Bruce. They were re-printed last year, and they were changed because of some comments which appeared in some early publications. These came out around 1910 and did no more than tell the truth, as the truth was told at that time. There were remarks about aboriginal people in them that were certainly derogatory - but it's how the people thought at that time, and fiction, you see, is an important part of history. Fiction is an historical document, because the fiction of a period captures the feelings and stories of that time. In her books, Mary Grant Bruce was telling us about Australia as it was then, about our attitudes at that time, about our stupidity at that time, about our frailty at that time. Those social attitudes were fact. But now we've got to change them.

BY CHANGING HISTORY YOU DENY THE FACTS. IT'S NOT EDITING, IT'S CENSORING.

If you read War and Peace *or* Anna Karenina *you will know that Tolstoy related, in fictional terms, a clear picture of what Russia was like. You get a genuine and accurate feeling for the Russia of Tolstoy's period by reading his books... and the same if you read Dostoevsky. Dickens, of course told us what England was like... William Faulkner and Harriet Beecher Stowe enlightened us on aspects of America, and so have all the great writers, of all their times and places. The world's most wonderful writers wrote the world's most wonderful stories, and all of them inspired by what? The piece being fiction is inspired by FACT... dear reader, that's what, FACT. Some of it might have been agreeable, some of it might have been horrible, some of it might have been cruel, some of it even bigoted, intolerant or sordid. Whatever it was, the author simply wrote of the way it was.*

We must not allow the supposed new thinkers, the people who I call the neo-vandals of our vocabulary, to

The Truth Stealers

censor and tamper with history by altering it in its printed form. Puerile publishers, petrified by the politically correct, explain they are simply editing material to update it. How, dear reader, do you update history without distorting it? I repeat: By adding to the truth you inevitably subtract from it. By changing history you deny the facts. It's not editing, it's censoring.

I imagine if we were to conduct a readers, poll to identify the most loathed man in history, Adolf Hitler would be at, or about, the top. You might care to recall Adolf Hitler's censorship. He just burned whole books. The world has never forgiven him, rightly so, for many things. But one of his most blatant acts of vandalism was the attempt to change history by destroying it in its printed form. Surely, we're not going to allow this nonsense so chillingly resonant of the nazis to get any sort of a foothold here in Australia? If we do, we should hang our heads in shame... which we'll do easily - because when

SOMETIMES IT'S NECESSARY TO BE ABSURD TO DEMONSTRATE ABSURDITY.

you have little backbone the head lolls forward of its own accord.

It's time to stop the vandalism of the vocabulary. The English language, in its purest form, is unquestionably art and it's in the process of being vandalised. The word "vandal", incidentally, is most appropriate when tied to vocabulary. The vandals, you see, were a barbarian tribe, best known for their blind savagery and their desire to destroy mainly one thing - works of art. They were on the scene in about the fifth century A.D. and what they left behind them was a trail of deliberate destruction. Their venom knew no bounds. Today we have the vandals of the 20th Century... and we must see that they don't last into the 21st Century. Our children are being robbed of the past and that's sinful and tragic.

Maybe some of you reading this are saying: "Laws, that's absurd"... Well, sometimes it's necessary to be absurd to demonstrate absurdity.

*'m so horny the crack of dawn
isn't safe.*
- K.M.

I never met a brave man
with a good imagination.

I have competed against many better than me but I remember one competitor who really *thought he was above me - and he was... until he had that thought.*

I spent most of my money on
booze and women; the rest I just wasted.
- J.S.

've had a lover's quarrel
with the world.

would like to live for a long time
but not if it means getting old.

I would vote for a woman for any position in private enterprise or government - but not any woman. Certainly it's great to see women get along but only if, as people, they deserve it.

If it's a serious judgement based on impulse, it ceases to be a serious judgement.

*If it's natural, it's easy.
If it's unnatural, it's difficult.
I've never met a man who found it difficult
to marry. I've never met a man who
found it easy to divorce.*

If I am in the middle of the road,
I deserve to be run over. Don't I?

If hypocrisy was bad for the environment, the world would have ended a long time ago.

The Equadorian Panama Hat

I was once roundly criticised for declaring that if you must buy a hat, buy a Borsalino - or better still a Montecristie Equadorian Panama. I was even labelled a traitor. What about Akubra, they asked? Well, Akubra is fine if you want to look different (like everybody else), but an endangered species it is not. Yes, I did say endangered species. While all the friends of fur and feather - the Bambi Brigade - are cluttering up our television screens, trying to save every remaining insect on the planet, the Equadorian Panama Hat is slowly sinking into oblivion. Unlike the Delhi Fly. In some parts of America you can be fined or gaoled for killing the Delhi Fly. How do you tell the difference between a Delhi Fly and any other? I don't know. Frankly I'd spray first and ask questions later.

Back to the hat. I'm the proud owner of a Montecristie Panama from Equador. I bought it in a little shop in Honolulu after maybe five or six "Bloody Mary's" at the Royal Hawaiian. My slight lack of sobriety obviously numbed my mind when I saw the price tag but with the hat came some information from the seller, some details I would like to pass on to you.

Why is a hat from Equador, not Panama, called a Panama I hear you ask? Well, in 1906 President Theodore Roosevelt went on an inspection tour of the Panama Canal. The black-banded hat he wore as he worked the steam shovel was the Montecristie Fino. Understandably because of where he happened to be, this prompted comment about the President's "Panama" hat - but these classics, dear reader, are certainly not made in Panama. They are made in Equador, in and around a little town called Montecristie.

As I've already said, President Theodore Roosevelt wore one, so did the other Presidential Roosevelt. Upper class Brits loved them too - George V, Edward VII, and others. Napoleon of France, Clark Gable in Gone with the Wind, Paul Newman, Charlie Chan. Charlton Heston wore one in The Naked Jungle. Do you remember Flamingo Road with Sidney

The Equadorian Panama Hat

Greenstreet? You certainly remember him in Casablanca. *Noel Coward almost lived in a Montecristie. Gregory Peck wore one in* To Kill A Mocking Bird *and so too, more recently Peter O'Toole in* The Last Emperor. *And me. So I'm in good company.*

Until you've seen or touched (no, fondled is a better word) an Equadorian Panama hat you can't possibly understand the beauty of this practical piece of equipment. Each hat is woven by hand if it's the real thing, and most of the work is done at night, between midnight and six in the morning, as the moisture of the night hours protects the fragile straw from damage. I have it on good authority that the one I am proud to own would have taken six to eight months to weave at night, the work done by one man - and the weaver no youngster, either.

A generation ago there were a couple of hundred people who could weave these hats. A generation before that the numbers were in the thousands. Today guess how many are left?.. Just 20.

Unless something happens, there may be none at all a generation from now. All the surviving weavers who create these extremely fine hats are well into their 70s and 80s. Manufacture of the hats will probably only survive as long as they do because, as is so often the case with the youth of today, nobody wants to learn.

Now, I have nothing personal against the Delhi fly which is currently on the endangered species list - but I'm sure an Equadorian Panama Hat has a lot more to offer the world. What's more, it won't spread germs.

If you're lucky enough to have one of these hats, keep it... it's a treasure and if you are lucky enough to travel, stop off in Hawaii and seek out a company called Kula Bay Tropical Clothing. Tell them I sent you, you might just pick one up. But just one word of warning - hold onto your hat when you ask the price!

*If it weren't for pickpockets,
I'd have no sex life at all.
- Al.*

*If the outdoors is so wonderful
how come the homeless don't like it better?*

*If they say it's public opinion, beware.
Public opinion is simply what everybody thinks
everybody else thinks.*

If we fail as citizens to keep our eyes wide open, we will in our time witness governments, particularly those with a socialist bent, become nothing more than money exchanges, transferring money from people who have earned it to people who haven't.

If you are on the way to the poorhouse try to pay the little bills before you get there.

*If you are very poor
you must be very polite; if you are very rich
you must be even more polite.*

*If you deliberately stand in
the way of another you also stand in
the way of yourself.*

*If you don't have the strength
of character to change your vote,
then you don't have the right to complain.*

*If you do what you like,
you're in trouble. If you like what you do,
you're a success.*

If you have made it to about 35 and your job still requires you to wear a name-tag - you have probably made a serious vocational error.

If you have nothing to say,
make sure you say nothing.
If you have something to say,
make very sure you say it in short sentences,
sharp and straight to the point.

Investment

 t would seem to me that if the economy is going to move in the right direction, we must get investing *to move in the right direction - towards more investment - to create jobs and expansion, more employers, more employees. You can't make the economy bigger by making the government bigger.*

YOU CAN'T MAKE THE ECONOMY BIGGER BY MAKING THE GOVERNMENT BIGGER.

To make the economy bigger surely you have to encourage concessions to expand the private sector. That way more people have more chance to create more wealth - and consequently the opportunity to employ more people. One of the basic tenets of irreverent logic is if you want more employees you must have more employers... simple isn't it?

If you have something important to say make sure you start at the end.

*f you have to start demanding love
you'll also demand hate.*

If you know everything *but are nothing then you are* absolutely *nothing.*

*If you prepare for something,
you will more than likely get it - like old age.
That's what worries me about countries who
insist it is morally right to prepare for war.
If you're prepared for fighting then you'll more
than likely find an excuse for a war.*

*f you purify the pond,
the lily dies.*

*If you really love her,
you'll keep seeing her in crowds
she's not even in.*

*f your eyes are full of love,
tears don't matter.*

If you want to keep the dream alive, don't sleep.

*If you really want to know where
God is - ask a drunk.*

If you want a friend you can really trust, if you want or need something you can unequivocally count on - try silence.

*If you want more employees,
you need more employers.*

Correctness

Is there anything more tedious than being in the company of someone who can only do the right thing? People are so concerned with correctness these days - rarely however is their concern based on how their behaviour will affect them and people around them.

It's simply that they choose to be proper so they will not be looked down upon, so they will be accepted. It has little to do with making others feel good, it has a lot to do with making themselves feel good. So, my advice is - raise a little dust now and again, breach the bounds of properness.

THE MAJOR ISSUE IS PERSONAL RESPONSIBILITY - THAT IS ACCEPTING RESPONSIBILITY FOR YOUR OWN MIND AND YOUR OWN ACTIONS.

The world is full of people who have views on all sorts of subjects, simply because they are seen by others to be the right *views* and the right *subjects*. Don't be grabbed by the mind and pulled around by others so that you end up thinking what the morally anointed think you, and all of us, should think - about the environment, abortion, homosexuality, social issues, freedom of choice, civil liberties, etc etc... ad nauseam.

The major issue is personal responsibility - that is accepting personal responsibility for your own mind and your own actions - even if those things happen to be outside the bounds of conformity.

Upside-down thinking beats lateral thinking any day and, apart from that, lunatic asylums are full of prissy, puritanical, priggish, prudish

Correctness

people who, afraid of dis-conformity, tortured their minds to such a degree that they snapped.

Don't be bedevilled because of what you do, just make sure you do what you can do now, I don't suggest for a minute that bad behaviour and sanity go hand

RAISE A LITTLE DUST NOW AND AGAIN, BREACH THE BOUNDS OF PROPERNESS.

in hand, probably far from it, but I do suggest that being constantly concerned about correctness will drive you mad if you are simply being correct to pacify people - while lying to yourself. Don't aim to be improper - but at least look as though you could be.

If you want to know how to talk,
first learn to listen.

*Be patriotic.
Join the army. Travel to exotic distant
lands, meet exciting unusual people...
and kill them.*

*If you're at a dinner party
and more than three people at the table say
I couldn't agree with you more, tactfully
throw up, get up and leave.*

If you're going to buy a hat buy a Borsalino or an Equadorian Panama. Why?... When you get it you'll know why.

*If you're miserable because
she hasn't told you everything,
you'll be more miserable when she does.*

*If you're young and can't cry,
you're a fool. If you're old and can't laugh,
you're a bigger one.*

*If you've got something to do,
you can bet your life that there's someone around
with nothing to do who will stop you.*

*Ignorance and stupidity are far
from the same thing... stupidity is incurable.*

Ignorance is not bliss.
Ignorance is ignorance.

In 218 B.C. Hannibal crossed the Pyrenees with one elephant – and got a mountain that never forgets.

*I*n a mind full of malice,
there's no room for reason.

Sickeningly Superior

f the middle class like it (by the middle class we mean the majority) no matter what it is - morality, old fashioned values, decency, barbecues, touch football, beer - it's then that the morally anointed dismiss *it*, act as though they are above it, and believe *they are above it*. If the majority like *it*, the morally anointed dismiss *it*. The self-elected elite look with disdain upon the major part of this country and its inhabitants and give no time to discussing the merits or otherwise of populist theories. They just mention them among their own crowd... and snicker. God help them and their inferior superiority. But because this elite group has power - and it does, make no mistake - it helps firm the policies of politics. You see politicians (with very few exceptions) pander to the elite, the morally anointed.

YOU SEE POLITICIANS (WITH VERY FEW EXCEPTIONS) PANDER TO THE ELITE.

Name any social issue and the elite are heard: poverty, abortion, morality (especially morality, including homosexual morality), AIDS, racial problems, mental illness, family values, welfare, law reform and so on and so on, please note, dear reader, all issues pertaining to the minority and government's think they are smart pandering to the elite. Well, we the middle class should teach them a lesson.

In the 1960's draft dodging was an accepted way of life (witness the President of the United States). In the '90s responsibility dodging is an accepted way of life, somebody else is always to blame. Mostly the government. Well, the government may be responsible for the mountain of debt but the debt does little to damage the next generation in comparison with the attitudes we leave our children.

JOHN LAWS' BOOK OF IRREVERENT LOGIC

*In the battle for rights,
commonsense is the first casualty.*

124

ntuition belongs to women.

nvest in your own future.

Irreverent logic has many more facets than conventional wisdom.

Irreverently logical facts:
- *Criminals are habitual liars*
- *Peace on earth is a myth*
- *Psychiatrists are professional sceptics.*

I smoke cigars;
I don't like the taste, but I enjoy the privacy.
Cigars clear rooms like a Yoko Ono album.
- Rene.

It is impossible to guarantee world peace, but it should be possible to guarantee world freedom.

It is not a crime to be rich;
it is not a crime to have influence.

It's true there is a fool born every minute; it's also true they don't die that fast.

*I*t's not what you say –
it's how sincere you can make it sound.

Bashing the Rich

here are still cries of "belt the rich" coming from the extreme left (where else) of the Labor party and from the bumbling Bishops of the Catholic Church. This group probably represents the last remaining vestige of true socialist mentality - the idiot culture. The rest of the world has woken up, but not the good old left wing - or the left-footers for that matter. They seem to have some sort of obsession with the top five percent of wage earners. The problem, in truth, lies in the bottom *five percent*.

It's extraordinary that even the lunatic left and the bumbling Bishops seem to accept the fact that super-stars get super pay - whether they be sports stars, film stars, or rock stars. But somehow they can't accept that the stars of industry, responsible for the employment of masses of others (have you ever met anybody who was paid by a poor man?), are entitled to large rewards.

To be perhaps a little callous, but totally truthful, it's not the top five percent that should be the concern of these allegedly "concerned" politicians - but the bottom five percent, this group being totally dependent on government handouts. What does the future hold for them, more of the same very likely, dear reader, more of the same.

It's a bad government that profits from keeping people sorry for themselves.

I*t's okay to miss your ex-wife...
so long as your aim is improving.*

It's been so long since I've had sex,
I can't remember who gets tied up.
- N.S.

It's crazy to think everybody hates you – not everybody knows you.
– J.L to A.J.

*Just because you can laugh
doesn't mean you can't tell the truth.*

*Just because there are two sides,
it doesn't automatically follow that you
have to be on one or the other.*

Like it or dislike it, approve or disapprove, men are sexually attracted to women.

Look a man in the eye and
say what you really think, instead of smiling
and saying what you're supposed to think.

Love is blind;
and what's more important
it's colour blind.

Make welfare as hard to get as a building permit and we'll all be OK.

*Make no mistake
- the last crocodile on earth would make
short work of the last animal rights activist.*

Memo Governments: Leave Us Alone!

f governments really wanted to do what was right for the people, they would leave them alone, particularly when the people have a craving not to be like *everybody else*, but to be better *than everybody else*.

People should be left alone to go about their business of achieving, employing, producing, and God forbid, making money. That, after all, is a healthy thing to do - to make money honestly with energetic application and effort.

Why can't government leave such people alone? They have broken no laws. All they seek is what humanity in the main seeks: Happiness, abundance and success. And they are not such bad things to seek, surely. But just try it! If, by trying hard enough you actually succeed through hard work and achievement, you'll find that because of the attitude of governments, what once was considered as "hard work" and

SENSES AND SENSIBILITIES ARE FREE, QUITE FREE, YOU DON'T GO OUT AND BUY AN INTRINSIC SENSE.

"achievement" becomes "selfishness" and "greed", suddenly, dear reader, if you happen to have done well, you are looked upon with growing scepticism, with disbelief. How did this happen? Someone must have left him money, they mutter.

"They", the mob, will seek to find some oblique excuse for you having achieved. It couldn't have been through hard work; it couldn't have been because you put your money at risk. Please note - your money, yes your money, dear reader, and yet they still cry... it's not fair. How dare you have money to put at risk. These attitudes are pushed by people who convince themselves all is not well in their lives - because of others. They are the takers of no personal responsibility. Governments will always prop up these sort of people, come to the aid of the unsuccessful - with, of course, the money of the successful. They will tell us all that they are investing in "welfare".

Memo Governments: Leave Us Alone!

Investing - *is government speak for spending. In my view they interfere with lives of people by destroying that which is natural in most of us - the desire to be happy, to achieve and be successful. By coming to the rescue of those who* can't *achieve and sometimes* won't *achieve, they are pilfering personal pride from people. They are, by stealth, undermining a basic human trait, a quality and virtue that exists within all humanity - self-preservation. This simple attribute can be said to have held society together. Now through government gratuity, communities crumble because of lack of self-esteem, because of the voiding of values such as self-preservation.*

Senses and sensibilities are free, quite free. You don't go out and buy an intrinsic sense. It's there already. Someone gave it to you - God if you like. It's something inbuilt in us all, yet we are allowing self-interest groups like governments and other failures

to destroy it. It's crazy. It takes no great effort, no great pain to encourage, to sanction something which cost us nothing. Self-sufficiency is a natural power, yet it has been eroded. Governments have worn away the rock of the human mind by a constant flow of excuses. And we have allowed them to encourage others to see themselves as victims... crushed, aggrieved, persecuted, depressed, deprived. The solution? Handouts - loot - government loot... the tax-payers' loot! It sounds simple. It is *simple and that's why the cerebral giants of Canberra do it.*

GOVERNMENTS DON'T WANT PEOPLE TO SUCCEED. IF EVERYBODY SUCCEEDS, THERE'S NO NEED FOR THEM TO INTERFERE WITH OUR LIVES.

They do it because it's politically expedient and because it keeps the people in the pay of the politicians. In their debt. Governments don't want people to succeed. If everybody succeeds, there's no need for them to interfere with our lives.

Isn't it our duty to remind those who feel they've been given a bad deal that they own unencumbered, lock stock and barrel, free of mortgage,

Memo Governments: Leave Us Alone!

the greatest resource on earth. The human mind. Shouldn't we encourage all people to lift themselves to strive to achieve to do all the things the majority take for granted? Of course, this is the way it should be, but governments rarely admit it. It's all too hard. It's so much easier to hand out the money of the workers to the non-workers. With it they get the warm inner glow of what they have the hide to call compassion. We know better, dear reader, we know better. This is no warm inner glow. This is the hot flash of power.

They want people to feel bad so that they can feel good. Why do people give to others, why do people give to charity? Because it makes them feel good. Sometimes even needed. Right there is the answer, people, right there is the answer. Governments give to encourage us to believe we need them. Look closely at those who say they need government support - are they happy, well adjusted, fulfilled, contributing? Of course not, dear reader, most are living in abject poverty, in depressed

conditions with depressed outlooks, hanging on to an existence - not a life - by the string attached to a government handout. Has the so-called generosity of governments made for happy people?

You know the answer. And there is no point in arguing with exceptions. There are always exceptions. You know the answer. Just look at those who have achieved - have a look now. Mostly they are happy, fulfilled, elated people, possessors of self-esteem and self-respect - and well able to be personally responsible.

GOVERNMENTS GIVE TO ENCOURAGE US TO BELIEVE WE NEED THEM.

I have no doubt that many who believe it's their right to encroach upon, or even their duty to involve them-selves in another family, are well intended. Then again, it's quite extraordinary how intentions escalate when they are fuelled with somebody else's funds. In all of this I am firmly of the belief that politicians generally have a much more sinister agenda - one designed in the main to enhance the apparent function of government.

ake sure somebody needs you.

an's education is never complete.
While you live, you learn.

*Many people convince themselves
that if it is economically necessary,
it's morally right. It's not always the case.*

*Men are destructive;
they make nuclear bombs. A woman would
never make a nuclear bomb that would kill you.
They would just make a bomb that made
you feel bad for a while.*

Most real women care more about the economic welfare of themselves and their families than they do about feminazi claptrap.

Murder is against the law,
and murder should be against the law.
But people murder people just the same. Reason?
The authorities don't exercise the law they already
have against the criminals they've already caught.
There's not much point in having the power to
make a law and lacking the strength to use it.

My favourite thing about school
was the smell of the books.

Never explain yourself.
Your friends don't need it and your enemies
won't believe it anyway.

Never position yourself so the cost of being defeated is greater than the advantage of winning.

Never accept a position just because it pays you well. Accept it because it pleases you well – then the pay will flow even more generously.

Never stand behind a horse,
or in front of a bureaucrat.

The Sacrifice

overnments are very good at asking people to make sacrifices. Fine. Just about any decent citizen would do that and maybe even feel good about it, if the sacrifice involved was for the country. But you and I, as practising skeptics, however, know a little more. Basically governments want us to sacrifice our money so that they can spend it. Wisely? Of course! Handing out free condoms for safe sex, rather than encouraging people to bear personal responsibility for their own actions. Campaigning against tobacco, rather than doing something positive about the illegal drugs.

Oh yes, the more we give them the more they want. Not so that we can feel good, just so they can feel good. These puffed up politicians are very good indeed at getting themselves on some sort of moral high by blowing our money.

No body of people,
no matter how well intentioned, can ever
conquer humanity's capacity to deceive itself.

Not wanting to go against human nature is neither prejudice nor bigotry.

Now, you don't mind giving a little more if it's to do good. But you do if it's simply so the government can do well.

Of course there are a lot of
bad things in history, nobody can argue that.
The books are full of acts of barbarism and
violence. The thing to remember is that
that truth is an indicator of just how much we,
as human beings, can put up with.

ne size doesn't fit all.
Nor will it ever.

Only humans don't treat animals like animals.

Opinion polls and minority groups
- right there is where the real danger lies.
Once, we knew what moral standards should be,
we knew that instinctively. Now instinct is
overruled by minority groups and opinion polls.
They tell us what the standards are - and many,
terrified at being seen marching to the wrong
tune or mincing to the wrong record,
go along with it all.

People *should not put themselves first.*
Governments *should put people first.*
Both *should put their country first.*

People talk despairingly about the alliance between the Australian Labor Party and the Australian Council of Trade Unions. This is understandable. No group, no matter how small or how large, can abide two leaders - especially when only one of them is democratically elected by the people. A country needs one strong leader who doesn't toil to be perfect. Choose him any day over a weak leader who thinks he is perfect.

olitical parties should not be simply a device to transfer money from people who have earned it to people who haven't.

Politicians are not renowned for their desire to create anything but votes.

Eating Soap Powder

hink about this: How many people are employed (using taxpayers' money) to ensure that labels are furnished with warnings that nobody reads. Too damn many, that's how many dear reader. Too damn many. It's the same old story of government interference - everywhere you turn there's another warning. And, do you know what? The more you see, the less you notice. It's called desensitising... getting used to it, in other words. These days we are just getting used to so much - because some bureaucrat has to warn us. Governments, you see, think we're too stupid, dumb, dense, doltish to know it's not a good idea to eat soap powder.

For kids, maybe it's different. But then the kid can't read the stupid warning anyway. Still it's another good way of wasting our money, and that's what the bureaucrats are best at.

Poor men are not thieves.
They may pilfer food or warmth but really
they are not thieves. Thieves are people who
have some *and want more.*
Poor men have nothing.

acism is not an excuse
for not even trying.

Rights are something that should be enjoyed by everybody *at a cost to* nobody, *no matter how rich and powerful or poor and underprivileged.*

Remember, equality is an impossibility. Nobody is equal to anybody. Even the same man need not be equal to himself on different days.

Remember, public ignorance
is government's best friend.

*Respect the source of life.
Also respect the ocean, the forests, and the stars.*

eek the truth.
How many times have you heard that one?
Seek the truth. Fine idea. Encourage it in people
but start looking yourself when others say they've
found it. As I've said before, sincerity is no
attestation of truth. Truth was what was sought
by the great minds... Aristotle, Socrates, Plato,
Samuel Johnson. They searched for truth by
interpreting the evidence. Today, too often ideology
and fanaticism stand in the way of truth.
Those who once were described as radicals are
today described as liberators; malicious malcontents
become instant visionaries. Their vision is not
obstructed by truth - they cannot see it.

Sex is one of the most beautiful,
natural and wholesome things money can buy.
-J.B.

hort people tan faster.

imple rule of the road:
Dumb drivers have the right of way.

*Sincerity is not much good
unless it's shackled to intelligence.*

The Pursuit of Excellence

e talk often, and we should, about government interference, particularly do-gooder government interference. I'm talking here about those governments who have been weak enough to have a few mandatory revolutionaries hanging around the place - people not vaguely interested in the pursuit of excellence *but* interested mainly in the pursuit of fairness.

These people expect the government to ensure that everything *is fair. Now,* anybody with any hint of brains understands that this is a total impossibility. Life itself is not fair, and if these imbeciles think they can make all things fair, they are wrong. All their meddling interference, taking, giving, is simply government intervention in our private lives - and a huge waste of money. I find it hard to come to terms with the audacity of these people -

with the hide, the egos of these people who seem to believe that we can't live without them.

Their motives are so good, so pure. They are the caring, compassionate, nice people. They want the equalisation of outcome. They want everybody to be treated the same way. They want business managed, they want incomes redistributed, but only, of course, by them. These people are running blind, arms outstretched, bumbling, stumbling in search of fairness. Meanwhile what everyone in this country should be doing is holding our heads high - striding out in our own determined search for excellence.

Have you noticed how government and the ineffectuals in it seem totally pre-occupied with those who fail - even to the point of blaming society

HAVE YOU NOTICED GOVERNMENTS SEEM TOTALLY PREOCCUPIED WITH THOSE WHO FAIL, EVEN TO THE POINT OF BLAMING SOCIETY FOR THEIR FAILURE.

The Pursuit of Excellence

for their failure. They rave constantly with their idealism, their pie-in-the-sky-ism, claiming that they are seeking equality. That's good, as we have all agreed on so many occasions, if it's equality of opportunity.

But they don't seek equality of opportunity. They seek equality of result. They seek to punish the achiever. Then they can enjoy equalised failure, equalised pain, equalised misery. These ratbags don't approve of individual excellence. If you have achieved, they can't wait to snipe away at it. What they represent is resentment in its purest form. The original French connotation of resentment is: "The passionate envy of the qualities and possessions of another, carried to the point of spite and hatred".

But even they can't stamp out individual excellence, because they can't stamp out human nature.

Standing against all they represent is the fact that we have all been created differently.

This government and its collection of do-gooders seem to seek out the obstacles that they believe to be the reasons for failure. They trot out all the tired old "newspeak": gender equality, lack of self-esteem, homophobia, sociopathological self-destruction etc. Keep focusing on obstacles and all you are going to get is more obstacles, more excuses, the fated failures of our world crying out I didn't do well because I lacked self-esteem - the government told me so. I have been a victim of homophobia - the government told me so.

All the government is doing is providing people with excuses to be failures and encouraging bitterness and hatred in the mushy minds of those who lack character. The government and its fellow travellers

WE MUST TAKE CARE OF THE ACHIEVERS - BECAUSE THE ACHIEVERS ARE THE PEOPLE WHO RAISE THE SIGHTS OF EVERYBODY.

The Pursuit of Excellence

are diluting talent and slowing down drive. Talent and drive, I remind you, are two of the most important things that made this country what it is.

In sport you can still get away with wanting to be better because by being better you make even the failures look good. It's one of the great things about sport. See how far you get when you try it in some other field of endeavour though.

KEEP FOCUSING ON OBSTACLES AND ALL YOU ARE GOING TO GET IS MORE OBSTACLES.

When will governments stop putting their energy into punishing achievers and making the failures feel good. We must of course take care of the genuine failures but we must take greater care of the achievers - because the achievers are the people who raise the sights of everybody. Never in two lifetimes would I be convinced that anybody feels good about failure... but I know, beyond any shadow of doubt, that success makes everybody feel good.

Sixty percent of something is better than 100 percent of nothing.

Smile if you are not wearing panties.

So long as you believe someone
hates you, you will be eminently hateful.
Hate is catching.

Socialism eats itself.
Private enterprise re-creates itself.

ocrates *didn't waste time watching television.*

ome people, particularly the do-gooders of society, are of the belief that no man should have caviar until every man has bread. I am of the belief that some men have to have caviar in order that all men can have bread.

*Someone said art is life
and the other way around. Nonsense
- at least as far as modern art is concerned.
Life is more sufferable.*

tart with a blank page
and a crowded mind.

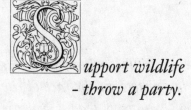

upport wildlife
- *throw a party.*

The environazis who want to
preserve every last insect on the face of the earth
want to stop - and stop dead - evolution.
The animals and insects have other ideas.
The dingo has scant regard for the
longevity of the rabbit.

The government shouldn't be elected on what you feel, it should be elected on what you think.

Unemployed

 t seems that if a company is on the brink of bankruptcy, it has a couple of choices: It can go broke, or it can work it's way back to a revived position. Surely its the same thing with a country.

I was reading just the other day about the United States in the 1930's under President Franklin Roosevelt. What they did was provide work for the out-of-work. I think we had a similar thing here but, of course, it's no longer politically correct to suggest that people who haven't got a job should be made to work.

This is what the "thought police" and "politically correct" who have swept this nation over the last five years, would like us to believe. But what is wrong with work for the out-of-work? What's wrong, dear reader, with a job when you haven't got one.

WHAT'S WRONG WITH A JOB WHEN YOU HAVEN'T GOT ONE.

In the '30s in America when the unemployed were employed, they built 650,000 miles of roadway - 125,000 public buildings - including 39,000 schools - 124 bridges - 8000 parks and 18,000 playgrounds. They also served over a billion meals to hungry school kids and sewed 382 million garments for needy people.

In this country we have children needing care, roads that need repair; bridges that need to be constructed - and yet we pay the unemployed poor to remain unemployed... and poorer still because they lose pride, self esteem and, most of all, the work ethic.

The only way to get out of any crisis is to work your way out, dear reader. We'd better start before we forget how.

he idea is not to avoid death,
but to enjoy life.

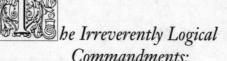

he Irreverently Logical
Commandments:

Never forget...
the value of time
the success of perseverance
the delight of working
the style of simplicity
the necessity of character
the power of kindness
the awareness of duty
the intelligence of economy
the virtue of patience
the joy of originating
the influence of example.

The lives of the black people will not be improved simply by denigrating the lives of the white.

The loudest voices on AIDS are not medical experts; they are the partners of AIDS sufferers, lawyers, judges and those with a special interest - but not medical experts. They bring bad tidings by way of the truth.

The morally anointed certainly rock
to the rhythm of a different sitar player.
Beware of them in politics. You would be safer
with a government made up of the first 20
names in any telephone directory than the
unlobotomised saviours – the Politically Correct.

The penalty for the perjurer
is that he ultimately believes the lie.

*The power to tax,
 in the wrong hands,
can become the power to destroy.*

The self-appointed thought gestapo are simply speed bumps in the traffic of truth, free thought and speech.

*The solution doesn't lie in
testing people for drugs or alcohol;
people should be tested for stupidity, illiteracy,
avarice and lust for power.*

The sometimes tortuous road of
experience will always lead to reality.

The suggestion that aboriginal people are in a worse state now than they were 30 years ago and the white people should feel guilty, is simply so stupid it could only be believed by a left wing intellectual - and there are some remaining.

Honesty

omebody faxed me recently a snippet from a Wall Street Journal - a pretty old Wall Street Journal, I suspect - but it was interesting. A couple of their better reporters were told to ask around and discover just how honest was the average person? What they did was pick out a bundle of common offences which even "respectable" people are more than likely to commit.

I doubt too many people would have a clean slate. In fact, I can't think of anybody I know who would have a totally clean slate and, at the risk of being abused for encouraging crime, I don't think I could abide the company of somebody who had never committed one of these offences.

Let me list them for you and give it a try. Just see how honest you really are:

- *Stealing Office Supplies*
- *Evading Taxes*
- *Illegal gambling*
- *Serving alcohol to minors*
- *Drinking in prohibited areas*
- *Possessing marijuana*
- *Possessing cocaine*
- *Engaging in prohibited sex acts*
- *Patronising prostitutes*
- *Shop lifting*
- *Driving while drunk*
- *Speeding*
- *Illegal Parking*
- *Lying to customs agents*
- *Lying on application forms*
- *Lying about jury duty*
- *Knowingly buying stolen goods*

JOHN LAWS' BOOK OF IRREVERENT LOGIC

Honesty

They are all things you shouldn't do and you'll find almost everybody you ask, if they are honest enough, may well be gone on five or six counts. The excuse? They are non-violent crimes; everybody does that; don't worry about it. That may well be right. Law breaking has been around as long as laws have been around. But just stop and think. If it were publicly noted that a member of Parliament was found indulging in any of these practices, chances are his career and working life would be over, finished, gone.

I can hear cries now, as I've heard them before: These people are put in high office and then break the law... politicians are crooks. The fact is, if you want to pursue it to that degree, we are probably all crooks. Did you pass the test?

If you're married with children aren't you in a pretty high office? You're a parent. That's more important than being a politician. And yet you expect the politician to be better than you. Funny old world, isn't it dear reader? Funny old world.

*The thought police will go to
any lengths to make any point, because they
convince themselves that they know better.
They will distort, manipulate, misrepresent and
even prevent the truth if they believe the cause is
good and of course, if it's their cause, it must be
good. But pray tell me how good is a cause that
requires distortion, misinterpretation,
misrepresentation and perversion
to make it believable?* Beware.

The trouble with being unaware that you are a fool is that you may believe you're smart.

he world is never fair.

The world would be different
if women were leaders. We wouldn't have
any wars - just some very severe negotiations
every 28 days.

*The worst thing about being
in a hurry is it takes such a long time.*

There are certain words in life you have to be aware of. Funding is one of them. It's a word generally used by bureaucrats or politicians who are terrified to use the word "money" but who are not too terrified to take it from taxpayers.

*here are many dangerous things
about propaganda. Keep in mind
propaganda is information designed to benefit
those who send it, not those who receive it.
Propaganda is not a good thing.*

There is a gaping abyss between good intentions and good results.

There is not a lot to be gained by getting to know someone too well.

*here is not one memorial
to a pessimist.*

There truly is nothing more beautiful than a truly beautiful woman. But aren't they hard to trust? You just know they have been getting away with murder most of their lives.

Achievements

 hat we all need to seek is the best possible outcome for everything. So you simply seek to escape from pain, seek the achievement of happiness, behave in a way that will allow you to avoid punishment, behave in a way that will entitle you to achieve just rewards.

THE IDEA IS NOT TO AVOID DEATH BUT TO ENJOY LIFE.

Australia shouldn't function on the basis of threats or fear. The idea is not to avoid death but to enjoy life.

These days the word tolerance as used
by the morally anointed simply means
that I have no right to object to what you do,
but you *have* a right to object to what I do
and what I think, or even what you think
I do and think.

These utopians generally dispute
what the majority credit as being proper
– whether it be moral behaviour
or social behaviour.

They were called the Dark Ages because religion reigned supreme.

This country is not in trouble
because the people are taxed too little.
It's in trouble because the government
spends too much.

Today's morality is just yesterday's immorality accepted.

*To begin with, most of us
have a love affair with a crowded life.
Companionship is paramount. Solitariness
never crosses the mind. As time goes on
be wise enough to consider the reverse:
Reclusion, with moderate amounts of diversity.*

*To be the head of the family
you don't have to sit at the top of the table.*

To lose doesn't necessarily mean
you've failed.

*Truth needs a little embellishment
to eliminate the boredom.*

*Try to be of good cheer –
not all the time – but ideally at the most
unexpected times.*

ry to be needed.

Job Funding

ever forget, dear reader, government's depend, largely, on public ignorance. Public ignorance is the best friend of the do-gooders - even do-gooding politicians - even "I would like to be" do-gooding Prime Ministers.

It seems to me that most people believe that a dollar out of Canberra en route to any other part of

PUBLIC IGNORANCE IS GOVERNMENTS' BEST FRIEND.

Australia can only come from tax revenue or from borrowing. So, which ever way it goes, the burden of the added debt falls to individual Australians scattered all over this wide brown land, God's great garden as we know it in the School of Irreverent Logic.

But remember what I said - public ignorance is governments' best friend. And that's all the more reason why you should keep asking questions.

We all die of something:
cancer, heart disease, stroke, motor car crash,
heart failure – but most people die from causes
other than AIDS. So why is more money per
capita being spent on AIDS research
than on any other?

We can't all be the same
and do the same thing. There must always
be a differing of opinions as there is a
differing of temperaments.

We need to remind ourselves, not infrequently, that if Captain Cook and his colleagues had decided to stay home, this place would simply be another third world calamity.

We want a leader who's not only a manager. We want a cheer-leader, hero-finder, builder, coach, enthusiast.

What a pity we don't pursue the salvation of humans with the same verve we pursue the salvation of animals.

What we really need to do is to keep homosexuals in the closet. But, dear reader, remember we should also keep heterosexuals in the closet, where most of them are anyway. Who for God's sake wants to hear about other people's sex lives.

What would you get if you crossed John Laws with James Dean? Answer: A rebel without a clue.
—B.R.

When a politician refers to
"every intelligent voter" he's referring to
the ones who vote for him.

When governments talk of sacrifice,
it doesn't for one moment mean sacrifice by
governments. It means sacrifice for governments.
You give up just a little more so they (the government) can have a lot more. It's government S.O.S.
- save our skins - and maybe, just maybe, there are
times when the people, for the sake of their countries
give more, only to be taught the hard way that
governments are masters of self-interest.
They give you extra as a way of buying votes.
Remember, the bottom line for politicians is votes.
Without them they're worthless.
Even with them many are still worthless.

*When people can dominate
governments, people won't need government.
Until such time, expect interference.
Lots of interference.*

When will the self-appointed superior beings who promote victimhood wake up to the simple fact that if there is one common trait in the makeup of the criminal mind, it is to blame somebody or something else for their own behaviour? Alcohol... now drugs... and we believe *them*. Criminals! *They are habitual liars and yet* we *believe them.*

Too Much Spending

 t's truth time again. A gentle reminder that this country is not in trouble because people are taxed too little. It's in trouble because the government spends too much.

Remember that welfare spending has increased from $1.56 billion to $28 billion in 20 years - an increase of 1054%. And that supporting mothers pensions 20 years ago - $40.5 million now risen to $3 billion - an increase of 7307%. And the population has increased by only 26%. Moral to the story?

Australia is not in trouble because the people are taxed too little but simply because the government spends too much.

AUSTRALIA IS NOT IN TROUBLE BECAUSE THE PEOPLE ARE TAXED TOO LITTLE BUT SIMPLY BECAUSE THE GOVERNMENT SPENDS TOO MUCH.

When you think:
'there is nothing that is really mine'…
remember your own thoughts.

*When you're successful,
it's easy to support individualism.
When you're not, it's easy to promote socialism.
When you're rich and successful -
take your pick.*

*While we search endlessly
for our so-called rights we lose sight
of commonsense.*

Who cares if women tell lies about their age: They only tell lies to other people and that's not dangerous. Men aren't quite that smart. They lie to themselves about their age and that's why you find all these galloots laid up with some sort of injury sustained in an endeavour that belongs to men of half their age.

hy are aboriginal activists
so easily offended? Simply because they are in
the business of being offended. It attracts attention
therefore it gains them special privileges.
Special privileges are not equality (to the contrary)
unless the special privileges apply to all,
then of course they would cease to be special
privileges. So it is that most governments take
the bloodline of least resistance, so to speak.
There is money in being offended.

Why do supposedly intelligent journalists constantly tell us that our esteemed politicians have hammered out a solution to the under-funding of some thing or another? Hammered out? It makes it sound as though there is actually something physically exhausting about spending someone else's money... our tax dollar.

*W*hy do the words "outraged" and "women's groups" always seem to go together?

hy is it that so many good looking women go to extraordinary lengths to avoid being seen as good looking?

ire coat hangers breed at night.

Women do it constantly -
it's a trade-off. They exchange freedom for security.
The voters should not be cajoled into doing the
same thing. You can't swap freedom for security.
All it means is the loss of freedom and security.

Women should not try to emulate men until men can be mothers and do a better job than the present incumbents.

W.A.S.P.S

f W.A.S.P.S decided to become involved in an historic review of their background (which in most cases would mean England) and celebrate these things, can you imagine the outcry?

Yet, the black people in this country are encouraged to dwell in their native cultures - as are immigrants to Australia - and we, if we don't accept this, are indirectly vilified and labelled racist. But really, is it healthy to be absorbed by the past - to dwell on the injustices, the cruelty, the tragedy that no doubt existed? Does it help to dwell on it?

I don't hear too many W.A.S.P.S complaining about the treatment of convicts - do you, dear reader?

ou cannot arrive at the truth by legislation. Because a government wants to have you accept something as being the truth does not make it so.

You can interpret history whatever way you like. You can interpret historical facts any way you like, providing you are not selective about the facts.

ou can never vote yourself richer.

You don't need a high education
to make your contribution. Simply be devoid
of hate, bitterness, prejudice, revenge and fear.
Got that? Fear. F.E.A.R.

ou never get rich on wages.

*You're only young once,
but you can be immature for ever... ask me.*

You need the open spaces for
rampant thought. Let them be big thoughts,
let them sail like a kite in the sky more than once
and when you finally wind in the string with a good
thought at the end of it, it will be tried and tested.
Big thoughts are not created in small places.